Hello, my name is Kathleen and here is my friend SUMO

Registration of copyright : 4th term 2016
National Library and Archives of Quebec
National Library of Canada
ISBN-13 978-2-9814968-1-2

Cataloging before publication at The National Library and Archives of Quebec and The
National Library of Canada

Contributors

Texts : Kathleen Desrosiers

Illustrations : Nathali Ruel

Page layout : Alexandre Tremblay

Translation: Anne-Marie Basch

Text editing : Amélie Bois et Chantal Brousseau

Contributor : Anne-Lise Paul

Original idea : Kathleen Desrosiers

A special thanks to Dr Joël Dehasse for his input. A very big thanks to the members of
my family for their support and advice, as well as everyone who read this book before
its publication and gave me their input.

To learn more about our publication or to obtain more information about our
copyrights, visit www.humanimo.org

INTRODUCTION

I invite you to follow our adventures to discover how Sumo and his canine friends communicate to understand them better. Sumo will guide you through an array of potential situations that could happen with your dog, your neighbour's dog or other dogs you encounter. You will learn to decode dog signals and to respect and act in a safe way with them. When you complete your apprenticeship, you will receive a canine language champion diploma! You can then teach your friends how dogs talk to us and how they communicate between themselves.

LET'S PLAY BALL

Joany and Dex play ball. Today Dex is a bit nervous.
He goes to lie down on the couch with his ball licking
his lips several times. Joany thinks Dex wants
some kisses.

I don't want kisses..... If
I lick my lips, it's because I would
prefer to stay alone to play
with my ball and this is
my way of telling you.

A LITTLE WORD FROM SUMO

When you see your dog licking his lips or the tip of his nose
repeatedly, he is telling you that he is
not at ease. At that moment, it is better
not to approach him and to leave him alone.
You can play with him later.

A STAY AT OUR GRANDPARENTS

Samuel is visiting his grandparents. He really wants to pet the little Enzo, grandpa's dog, but his tyrannosaurus appearance frightens him.

I look away and I bare my teeth.
It is a sign that I'm afraid.
I feel cornered and I have no escape.
Samuel better not approach me
because I could bite him.
I'm not mean, I'm afraid.

A LITTLE WORD FROM SUMO

When you see a dog in someone's arms you shouldn't approach it. It is better in this situation if the person places their dog on the ground so the dog feels free to escape. Then, you can pet it if it comes towards you.

A STARTLED AWAKENING

Dex is napping on his cushion in the corner of the living room. Samuel, who is playing, drops his ball and it rolls very fast beside Dex startling him awake!

> A rolling object speeding towards me and a running child!
> Will I be attacked?
> Am I in danger?
> What's going on?

A LITTLE WORD FROM SUMO

When you see a dog frozen, not moving, licking his nose and turning his head averting his eyes, he is telling you he feels insecure. When a dog is in the corner of a room or when he is sleeping it is better if you don't approach him to prevent frightening him. Instead get an adult to help you.

A VISIT AT NATHALIE'S

The whole family is visiting Aunt Nathalie. She has a beautiful dog named Angie. Angie has not been around children very often so she hides under the coffee table in the living room and stares at the wall. Gabrielle wants to rescue Angie, because she believes she is stuck under the coffee table. But BEWARE! I don't think it's the best solution.

I am not stuck under the coffee table at all! I was hiding because I have rarely seen little humans like you. I tell am afraid this little girl could hurt me because she moves very fast.

A LITTLE WORD FROM SUMO

When a dog is under furniture or under a table, you should not approach him. The best way to react is to wait for him to come out of his hiding spot by himself when he feels safe. You can also, with the help of an adult, toss little treats towards him so he starts trusting you.

AT LAST WE'RE BACK

Joany, Gabrielle and Samuel are back from a weeklong stay at their grandparents' house. They missed Dex and Kyra very much. Samuel approaches Dex and squeezes him very hard in his arms.

I am happy to see you too but I would like it much more if you scratched me under my chin instead of suffocating me.

A LITTLE WORD FROM SUMO

You should never squeeze your dog or any other dog. Dogs don't like feeling trapped in someone's arms and they can strike by biting or scratching you if they feel scared. The best way is to wait until the dog comes to you and then let him leave when he feels like it.

A BABY IN THE HOUSE

Our little cousin Chloe is visiting our house. She is still a baby, so she crawls around the house. She crawls very fast towards Kyra because she thinks she's cute. Kyra, who yawns repeatedly, is worried.

Who is this little human crawling on the ground very fast, coming towards me?

A LITTLE WORD FROM SUMO

A dog who yawns repeatedly is telling you that he is afraid or worried. If you see a toddler approaching a dog, immediately tell an adult so they can supervise the baby. It is always better to be cautious even if a dog is friendly.

YOU WANT TO TAKE MY BONE AWAY

Gabrielle approaches Kyra who is chewing on a bone. Kyra turns her head and averts her eyes. Gabrielle thinks that Kyra saw something in the other room. Finally, Gabrielle understands that Kyra would like to relax so she doesn't come near.

WELL DONE Gabrielle! You understand that it's my bone and that I don't want you to come near me because I'm afraid you will steal it from me. If I turn my head away like that, it is to make you understand that I would rather be alone to chew on my bone.

A LITTLE WORD FROM SUMO

When a dog eats his meal, a treat or is chewing on a bone, you should leave him alone and come back when he's finished.

THE NEIGHBOURS VISIT

Joany's little neighbour friends come for a visit.
When they see the cute little dog, they run at full
speed towards him. They want to play with him but
Kyra backs up. Joany understands quickly that
Kyra is afraid of them. She then explains to her
friends to wait until Kyra decides to come to them
when she feels more comfortable.
WELL DONE Joany!

Thank you Joany for explaining
how I feel! I don't know them
and they startled me! I will come
and see them a little later.

A LITTLE WORD FROM SUMO

When a dog's ears are bent back and his tail is low and
he is shaking, he's telling you he's afraid. In that
case, with adult supervision, you can toss
little treats towards him to let him know
that you don't want to hurt him. Even if he
eats the treats, you wait for the dog to
come to you without forcing him.

HOORAY! WE'RE PLAYING TOGETHER!

Samuel calls Dex over playfully. Dex comes charging and gets into a play position. Samuel throws the ball, he understand that his friend wants to play with him. Well done Samuel! You now understand dog language!

HOORAY! HOORAY!
We play together!
Throw me the ball, Samuel! You'll see how good I am at playing fetch!

A LITTLE WORD FROM SUMO

When a dog gets into this position, it is because he is in a playful mood: you can then play with him without worry.
Ask an adult to supervise while you play fetch with him anyway. It is better to be cautious because a dog can easily get overly excited.

FOUR STEPS TO APPROACHING

STEP 1

ASK THE GUARDIAN'S PERMISSION

You should always ask permission from the dog's guardian before you pet him. If the guardian is not there, never approach the dog, even if you know him!

STEP 2

ASK THE DOG'S PERMISSION

To ask the dog's permission, hide your thumb inside your fist. Then place your fist in front of you but not under the dog's nose! Just in front of your tummy!

A DOG SAFELY

STEP 3

LET THE DOG SMELL YOU

You should wait for the dog to come to you and let him smell you. It's up to him to decide if he wants to come to you or not. If he backs up or turns away, let him leave. It's a question of respect!

STEP 4

SCRATCH THE CHIN

Once the dog comes to you to smell you, bring your hand GENTLY forward and scratch under his chin. Never pet a dog on top of his head!

I FEEL GOOD, YOU CAN PLAY WITH ME OR PET ME GENTLY. I LIKE IT WHEN YOU ARE CALM AND GENTLE WITH ME.

Pet me please

I am calm

I am happy

I want to play

I AM WORRIED, AFRAID OR STRESSED. I PREFER TO BE BY MYSELF.

I lick my muzzle repeatedly

I yawn often

I raise a leg

I turn my head or look away

I AM VERY AFRAID OR ANGRY.

I am afraid that you will hurt me

I am very scared

I am terrified

ABOVE ALL DO NOT APPROACH ME.

I am barking while lunging forward

The hairs on my back stand up

I am barking in a crouching position

CONGRATULATIONS!

YOU NOW UNDERSTAND HOW DOGS
COMMUNICATE WITH US! SUMO
INVITES YOU TO DOWNLOAD
AND PRINT YOUR DIPLOMA AT:

humanimo.org/en/diplome

OUR STORY

My name is Kathleen Desrosiers, I worked for over 20 years in the animal field as animal health technician and also as a canine behaviorist.

Every year, too many animals are abandoned because of behavior and aggression problems. In 2008, I founded the Aïkiou company whose goal is to design innovative products that help prevent eating disorders and boredom.

After several years, my husband Alexander joined me at the head of the company in order to continue the mission we were given. Reduce dropouts by providing products that provide a stimulating activity for pets to fill their natural needs.

While my husband took the direction of the company, I decided to fulfill my dream. Writing my first book for children to help them better identify the canine language.

Like many families with pets, we were in search of educational tools to share our knowledge with our two daughters to make their relationship with our dogs safer.

Given that most bites are caused by the family dog, we needed a tool that can allow our children to learn to identify the different signals used by dogs to communicate with us.

FONDATION
HUMANIMO

AïKIOU

So we decided to create this first book of stories that makes it easy to teach in a fun way how to behave with dogs and prevent the risk of bites.

Thus was born the Humanimo foundation in 2014 with an educational mission with children and their families. We invite you to share the contents of this book with your children to help us in our mission.

Together, we will succeed in reducing the risk of bite and abandonment.

Thank you for your help!

Gabrielle, Joany, Kathleen, Alexandre, Dexter, Kyra

STATISTICS

« According to a Léger Marketing survey done in 2010 from the Association of Veterinary Medicine in Quebec, in partnership with CDMV and Hill's Pet Nutrition, in Quebec, 45,000 children 12 years of age or less were bitten by a dog in the previous 12 months, which represent a little more than 120 bites per day. The family dog is responsible for these bites at a rate of 38%. » (1)

In the United-States

« In the United States, each year, 4.5 million people are bitten by a dog. One child out of two is bitten by a dog before the age of 18. 359,223 children from 1 to 14 years of age were bitten between 2010 and 2012 (37% of those were between 5 and 9 years of age). » (2)

This shows the importance of implementing educational programs that teach children how to understand dog language in order to be safe around them. Children will then develop a better relationship with their canine friends.

References:

(1) http://www.newswire.ca/fr/story/658229/au-quebec-au-cours-de-la-derniere-annee-environ-45-000-enfants-ont-ete-victimes-de-morsures-de-chiens
(2) https://www.avma.org/Events/pethealth/Pages/Infographic-Dog-Bites-Numbers.aspx#.U3NmF1jNDX0.facebook